CHINESE FESTIVALS

The Dragon Boat Festival

Edited by Li Chaodong

Translated by Katie Xiaoshuang Xu and Bella Kexin Chen

Books Beyond Boundaries

ROYAL COLLINS

The Dragon Boat Festival, also known as Duanwu Festival, falls on the fifth day of the fifth lunar month and is one of China's four most significant traditional festivals. In September 2009, the Dragon Boat Festival was inscribed on UNESCO's *Representative List of the Intangible Cultural Heritage of Humanity*, becoming China's first festival to be enlisted as a world intangible cultural heritage.

The Dragon Boat Festival has multiple names and diverse festival events, among which the focus of most celebrations involves eating *zongzi* (rice dumplings) and holding dragon boat races.

The Dragon Boat Festival

Wen Xiu (Tang Dynasty)

Whose honor marks the Dragon Boat Festival fete?
Qu Yuan alone, as ancient tales, state.
Chu River's might, how it defies,
Loyal's grievances, unwashed and wise.

Despite its many origins and legends, the Dragon Boat Festival is now acknowledged and celebrated by most Chinese in memory of the patriotic poet Qu Yuan.

Qu Yuan, a noble of Chu State during the Warring States Period (476–221 BC), showed his rare talent in governing the country when he was young. King Huai of Chu trusted and valued him very much and often discussed state affairs with him.

However, Qu Yuan's forceful advocacy in his reforms met with rejection from the Chu aristocracy. He suffered from long-term exclusion and entrapment and was eventually demoted by the King Huai of Chu.

During his time in exile, Qu Yuan wrote long poems called "Li Sao" (The Lament) to express his concern for the country and its people.

Following Qu Yuan's exile, political corruption ran rampant in the court of Chu, leading to frequent defeats in battles against Qin. In 278 BC, the Qin Army conquered Ying, the capital city of Chu, and Chu was forced to cede territory for peace.

Hearing the news that his homeland had been invaded, Qu Yuan was heartbroken. He came to the Miluo River and touched a stone beside the river, thinking that the stone was clean without being trampled by the soldiers and horses of Qin State. Finally, strapping the stone to himself, Qu Yuan plunged into the roaring Miluo River. That day happened to be the fifth day of the fifth month in the Chinese lunar calendar.

Having heard about Qu Yuan throwing himself in the river, the local villagers flocked to the river and set out their fishing boats to look for Qu Yuan's body.

However, Qu Yuan's body could not be found. Consequently, the villagers threw lumps of rice into the river so that the fish would eat that rice instead of eating his body. Fearing that the rice balls would be eaten by the dragons in the water, people came up with another idea of wrapping rice in reed leaves and tying the leaves with five-colored silk thread. And these are traditionally held to be the origin of dragon boat races and *zongzi* as the food during the festival.

The Dragon Boat Festival carries spiritual connotations that transcend time to reflect Chinese people's unwavering patriotism.

More than 2,000 years have passed, but Qu Yuan, who was concerned about the country and the people, is still alive in people's hearts. Every year on the fifth day of the fifth lunar month, people eat *zongzi* and hold dragon boat races to commemorate the great patriot, reminding them to love their motherland. The government officially recognized the Dragon Boat Festival as a public holiday in 2007.

It is said that the Dragon Boat Festival is a festival for sacrificial purposes. Instead of saying, “Happy Dragon Boat Festival,” people should say, “Stay safe and sound at the Dragon Boat Festival.”

On the fifth day of the year, the lunar calendar marks,
The Dragon Boat Festival, a celebration with sparks.
Dragon boat races held in the shimmering water,
Welcoming new women home, a joyful matter.

—Anonymous

The Dragon Boat Festival carries Chinese people's love and respect for the family.

Guining (mothering) is another custom of the Dragon Boat Festival. On this day, married daughters, in a spirit of gratitude, come back to their parent's home. In ancient times, a daughter lived in her husband's house for a long time after getting married and rarely saw her parents. So daughters take the Dragon Boat Festival as a valuable opportunity to visit their parents at home. Thus, the Dragon Boat Festival is also called "Daughter's Day."

The Dragon Boat Festival expresses people's care for life as well.

The Dragon Boat Festival is also known as the "Health Festival" since ancient times, for many of its customs express people's care and respect for life.

During the Dragon Boat Festival, hanging Chinese mugwort and calamus is one of the important elements of the festivities. The special smell of mugwort and calamus can keep away mosquitoes, flies, insects, and ants and make the air cleaner. It can also help with feeling less cold and damp, feeling more refreshed, easing discomfort, strengthening bones, and getting rid of stagnant energy.

Collecting herbs is one of the oldest customs of the Dragon Boat Festival. The Dragon Boat Festival is also recognized as the only festival to promote traditional Chinese medicine in the folkways. On the fifth day of the fifth lunar month, according to folk customs, it is high time when *yang qi* (positive life energy) is at its most potent, marking a point when the medicinal qualities of herbs and plants are strongest. And people often go up the mountain to collect Chinese medicinal herbs before dawn on that day.

It is a custom to drink *xionghuangjiu* (realgar wine) during the Dragon Boat Festival. There is an old saying that "Drinking realgar wine drives diseases and evils away." So tradition has it that drinking realgar wine can not only dispel poison and ward off disasters but also protect health and bring fortunes.

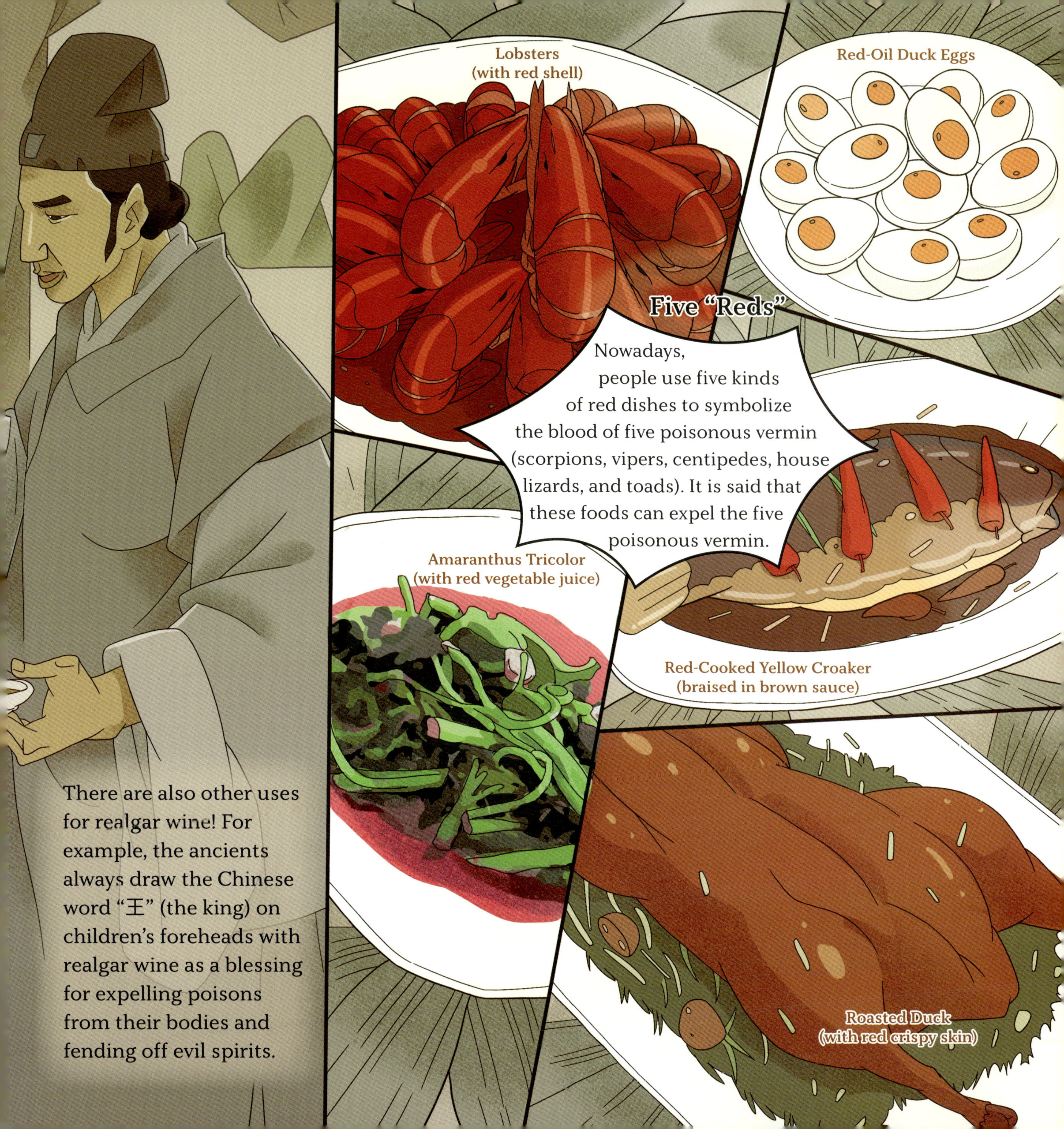

There are also other uses for realgar wine! For example, the ancients always draw the Chinese word "王" (the king) on children's foreheads with realgar wine as a blessing for expelling poisons from their bodies and fending off evil spirits.

During the Dragon Boat Festival, parents typically dress their children up with a perfume satchel to ward off evil. The sweet-smelling sachet, filled with cinnabar, realgar, and aromatic herbs, is usually wrapped with silk cloth, and then strung with colorful silk thread as decorative tassels. The sachet, which is delicate and lovely, is usually hung around the child's neck or tied to the front of his or her garment as an ornament.

Perfume Satchel
Ingredients
Aromatic
Cinnabar
Realgar

When it comes to the Dragon Boat Festival, the chewy and glutinous *zongzi* are often the first to be mentioned by Chinese people.

But you know what? There is a major difference in *zongzi* between Northern and Southern China in terms of flavor.

People in Northern China prefer sweet *zongzi* to savory ones.

Shandong Yellow Rice Zongzi

It is made of sticky yellow rice and packaged with dried jujube fruit, the Chinese red date. And *zongzi*, which tastes bland, can be dipped into sugar to increase the sweetness.

Xi'an Cold Honey Zongzi

The "cold honey" *zongzi* originated in the Tang Dynasty (AD 618–907). According to records, Wei Juyuan, who was the Prime Minister of the Tang Dynasty, hosted a dinner party for Emperor Zhongzong. The dinner was called "Shaowei Yan," and it was held to celebrate those who had passed the civil service exams during the Tang Dynasty. One of the dishes served at this dinner was called "Cifei Hanxiangzong." Its feature is "honey pouring," meaning to pour honey on *zongzi*.

It contains unique fillings of glutinous rice and red beans mixed with chili powder, Sichuan salt, monosodium glutamate, and cured meat, which makes the *zongzi* taste spicy and palatable with a unique flavor.

Zongzi from Southern China are both salty and sweet, but mainly salty.

In a rectangular shape, Jiaxing *zongzi* can be stuffed with fresh pork, sweet bean paste, eight treasures, chicken, etc.

The filling is a mixture of glutinous rice and marinated pork, mushrooms, dried shrimp, lotus seeds, marinated meat soup, white sugar, etc. Served with garlic paste, wasabi, chili sauce, sour radish, and other condiments, it tastes sweet, tender, and fatty but not greasy.

Celebrating the Dragon Boat Festival by eating *zongzi* is a tradition in China that has stood the test of time. It is also spread to the Democratic People's Republic of Korea, Japan, and other Southeast Asian countries.

It looks like a small torch.

It is wrapped in a square, like a package.

Does it look like a pillow?

Dagao (Glutinous Rice Cake)—Yanbian, Jilin Province

Mix mugwort with glutinous rice in a big wooden trough made of a single block of wood and beat them with a long handle wooden hammer.

Zongzi is not the only festive snack in China. Different regions across the country have quite distinctive dishes for celebrations.

Saozi Noodles—Qishan, Shaanxi Province

For people from Northwestern Shaanxi Province, the Dragon Boat Festival is incomplete without a bowl of saozi (minced or diced meat to bc added to noodles or other food before serving) noodles. Qishan County, in particular, is the most famous place for the dish. Qishan saozi noodles feature thin, smooth, and chewy noodles with chili oil floating on the soup surface and the soup tastes sour, spicy, and delicious.

Pancake—Wenzhou, Zhejiang Province

A piece of translucent cake in the shape of a full moon and thin as silk, with mung bean sprouts, leeks, shredded meat, shredded eggs, mushrooms, and other fillings placed on, is then rolled up to a wrap. When you eat it, you will taste a variety of different flavors in one bite.

Mung Bean Cakes

The mung bean cakes, with the function of clearing heat and cleansing, are also one of the necessary foods for the Dragon Boat Festival. The flavor of mung bean cakes is varied between Northern and Southern China. That is, mung bean cakes from the North are the Beijing style, which tastes fluffy as they are typically made with no grease added. Whereas those in the South are Suzhou and Yangzhou style, which need to be added with oil when making, and the taste is soft and delicate.

Broad Beans

Adults will also string cooked broad beans into necklaces and hang them on children's necks.

Eating Fish

During the Dragon Boat Festival, people in Taicang and Jiading areas in the south of the Yangtze River, rich or poor, will eat drumfish, commonly known as yellow croaker. And in Yizheng, Jiangsu Province, there is also an old saying that goes, "Pawn one's pants to buy yellow croaker."

Wudu Cake (Five-Poison Cake)

Wudu cake is the unique seasonal food of the Dragon Boat Festival in Northern China. The early summer of each year is the time when insects are in their peak reproduction season. Therefore, the ancients eat the “wudu cake” to pray to drive away diseases and strengthen their bodies.

The “wudu cake” is not really stuffed with “five poisons” but covered with patterns of the five poisonous vermin on the cake skin. The fillings commonly used are apricot paste, jujube paste, braised pork, mung bean paste, black sesame, etc. If no special attention is paid to the color of the fillings, they can also be made into flower cakes with roses alone.

CHINESE FESTIVALS

The Dragon Boat Festival

Edited by Li Chaodong
Translated by Katie Xiaoshuang Xu and Bella Kexin Chen

First published in 2023 by Royal Collins Publishing Group Inc.
Groupe Publication Royal Collins Inc.
BKM Royalcollins Publishers Private Limited

Headquarters: 550-555 boul. René-Lévesque O Montréal (Québec) H2Z1B1 Canada
India office: 805 Hemkunt House, 8th Floor, Rajendra Place, New Delhi 110 008

ISBN: 978-1-4878-1152-5

To find out more about our publications, please visit www.royalcollins.com.

ABOUT THE EDITOR

Li Chaodong, born in 1963, graduated from the Department of History of East China Normal University. He is a famous education publisher in China. He has edited and published more than 50 sets of books. He has won the title of "National Leading Talent in Press and Publication" and "China's Annual Publication Figure." He is the Founding Vice President of the All-China Federation of Industry and Commerce Book Industry Chamber of Commerce, Vice President of the Fifth Council of the Books and Periodicals Distribution Association of China, Vice Chairman of Anhui Publishing Association, and Vice Chairman of Jiangsu Publishing Association.